WHAT'S AFTER MAKING LOVE

Sharon Charde

Fernwood
PRESS

What's After Making Love

©2025 by Sharon Charde

Fernwood Press
Newberg, Oregon
www.fernwoodpress.com

All rights reserved. No part may be reproduced
for any commercial purpose by any method without
permission in writing from the copyright holder.

Printed in the United States of America

Cover and page design: Mareesa Fawver Moss
Cover image: Margarita Zueva
Author photo: Hedi Charde

ISBN 978-1-59498-183-8

For John, again and again

In this meditative, exquisite collection, poet Sharon Charde mines the depths of private grief to show how such experiences lend a kind of clarity to daily living. In *What's After Making Love* Charde offers a survey, an inventory of a life, with notions both practical and metaphysical: marriage, ticket stubs, beetles on a rosebush, the loss of a mother and a son. We are more than these things, Charde tells us, but only if we allow ourselves to be held in our sadness. That is the hard work of living, made lighter by the magic of a book like this.

—Alison Powell,
author of *Boats in the Attic* and *The Art of Perpetuation*

In these urgent poems, Sharon Charde grapples with the complex realities of a long life, the devastating death of a son, and the questions that arise from a restless intelligence trying to make sense of her often conflicting desires. The language of that search is intensely alive, the imagery haunting, and the grace that can be achieved is hard won. "What's after / making love?" A deeply moving portrait of one survivor, which has profound lessons for us all.

—Kathryn Levy,
author of *Reports* and *Losing the Moon*

In this collection of poems rich with metaphors of hunger and desire, Sharon Charde renders the ache of not living up to her parents' American Dream, the devastation upon losing a child, and the search for self within the bonds of long marriage. We feel at one with her when, dropping sticky rice into a monk's begging bowl, we realize that "the ordinary pie life gives" can provide enough sustenance after all.

—Kathryn Jordan,
author of *Riding Waves*

Fierce love, piercing grief, and the lyricism of resilience thread through Sharon Charde's memorable *What's After Making Love*, a book of poems that thrums with the truth behind family, landscape, and memory. "I bartered for this jagged, glossy liberty," says the speaker of Charde's poems, which sparkle with a wise and unforgettable voice. What does it mean to have "asked too many questions?" And also to unearth the roots of this asking? "I'm from all those questions and some of the answers," Charde's speaker reveals in poems that question authority while mothering, grieving, loving, and facing the present and what's to come. *What's After Making Love* locates renewal in language that sings, even though "The world is breaking / and I'm breaking with it."

—Tyler Mills,
author of *The Bomb Cloud* and *Poetry Studio: Prompts for Poets*

And think not you can direct the course of love,
for love, if it finds you worthy,
will direct your course.

—Kahlil Gibran

Contents

WHAT'S AFTER MAKING LOVE 13
One. 15
   PAPER DOLLS 16
   RESCUE 18
   NORA DENNIS IS PRAYING FOR ME 19
   ANOTHER MOTHER 20
   THE FATE OF ROMANCE OVER TIME 21
   WHERE I COME FROM 22
   THE NUNS TAUGHT US THE PERFECTION OF A
      MARTYR'S DEATH 23
   LINES 24
   RESHUFFLE 25
   ANGLE 26
   COOKIES 27
   CHIAROSCURO 28
   EVERYBODY DOESN'T
      GET EVERYTHING 29
   ASHES 30
   REMAINS 31
   NO ANSWER 32

- TO THE VERY END 33
- TIGER'S NEST HIKE, BHUTAN 2017 34

Two. 35
- NIGHTFALL 36
- I'm sorry for your loss 38
- SHOULD HAVE 39
- ABOUT THIS TIME OF YEAR 40
- FOOL 42
- VERSIONS 43
- THERE IS ALWAYS A WOLF 44
- BEHIND US 45
- THINGS 46
- DEATH 47
- CASUALTY 48

Three. 49
- For the longest time 50
- THE WAY IT WAS 51
- RECKONING 52
- FAMINE 53
- LISCANNOR, 2018 54
- ODE TO IRELAND 55
- WIFE 56
- WIFE, AGAIN 57
- HOSTAGE 58
- NEED TO EXHALE 59
- THE ELECTRICIAN 60
- THE BOSS CHOOSES ME 62
- why 63
- SIMULACRUM 64
- STICKY RICE 65
- ALMOST 66
- I KNOW YOU CAN'T HEAR ME 67
- THE THINGS I CARRY 68

CAN THIS MARRIAGE BE SAVED?	69
ECLIPSE	70
DONE	71
JUST THIS FACT	72
NO ONE'S GETTING ANYTHING RIGHT EXCEPT THE TREES	73
COMPOST	74
THIRD AGE	75
ANSWER	76
Acknowledgments	77
Title Index	79
First Line Index	82

WHAT'S AFTER MAKING LOVE

I've traded my pretty body enough to know.
At first it was easy. I had the map, knew,

in a general way, the geography—
apartment, child, house, his job, cook, clean, sew.

Pregnancy made my long hair shine.
The children wheezed and wrangled,

threw bricks at the barn windows
the August day I drove to New York

in the Volkswagen squareback, met him
at the apartment over Giambelli's on Fifth.

I could hear the music of women in lofts
downtown, but I wanted to drink gin with a man.

Braids, leather sandals, a flowered dress.
He gave me the key, but I sent it back.

I tried again with brown bread, no bra,
a different soup made every night.

Little white pills taken for twenty-eight days.
I looked at my clitoris in a mirror, the blue-

pink fleshy folds of it, spread out to Crosby,
Stills and Nash. I had a Superman shirt.

The boys had homework. We lived in a white
house, green shutters, treehouse in the back,

tractor in the barn. I canned tomatoes
from the garden. Our sheep Judith was

tethered there. Dogs roamed. We didn't
hear the guts-torn end the night they found

her. Sheep need shepherds. The melody
of some imagined party no longer calls me.

Everything I see is not nailed to a heavy
wooden cross. What's after making love?

The edges of a room long vanished. Outlines
of absence, a stone in your voice, blood

on the floor. God's teeth in my shoulder.
Your face. His death. Grace.

One.

PAPER DOLLS

Mother dropped me
at Mr. Blake's, went

to buy gin. Freed from
the Packard's back seat,

I push open the dense
wood door. Mr. Blake,

face cratered like a geode,
moves toward me.

Long tables stretch
behind us in dark

formation, pyramids
of pencils, glue, needles,

irons, yoyos, hammers.
I stand in his smell.

Hello, little girl. Paper dolls?
I've got some new ones.

He beckons me to the high
racks. Together we find flat

families smiling
page after page,

their clothes lined
up in neat parades.

How I loved their exactitude!
At home I slice outfits

carefully off the pages
for the naked

dolls, cut along
the tabs' little broken

black lines, bend
the dress on the mother,

the suit on the father,
and, just as they

taught me, leave
the children for last.

RESCUE

I do want to be loved, to become
the subject of my own life, but
I never had a brother, and my mother
didn't know how to love me though
she tried, *it's okay, don't worry* she said
when I called crying, lost the twenty
in Grand Central. *I'll wire you more.*
I spent a lot of time on my knees
back then, *Ad deum qui laetificat
juventutem meam*, to God who gives
joy to to my youth, no joy in our house—
Quia tues Deus fortitude mea—for Thou,
oh God, art my strength—maybe
praying would bring it—but better,
a brother who could have pierced
our girl-miasma, a protector, a curiosity,
an entertainment, made our dull family
glisten. *He* could have saved me. But
mother, father needed us fragile, a son
would be strength they couldn't
comprehend. They did want one, though,
my name was going to be Anthony.
Mother didn't believe she could birth
a girl—can you believe it? *Lord,
have mercy*, they may have said.
They got me instead.

NORA DENNIS IS PRAYING FOR ME

Every day, she says. I want to say
I'm praying for you too like we did
in high school, but I surrendered
that ritual years ago. Instead I laugh
and say *God would never hear a plea
from me*, but she just smiles, assures
me she would call the priest if I was
dying, and he would give me *the last
rites,* and now I'm laughing harder but
suddenly thinking about dying—after all,
I'm eighty. Will I be afraid? Will it be
quick? Or will the time before spin out
slowly, life unsure of when to leave?
I used to be as certain as Nora Dennis
is that there's a God waiting to welcome
a dead me, but belief became a tyranny
I bartered for this jagged, glossy liberty.

ANOTHER MOTHER

sang with Frank, knew the words
baked apple pies
jelly rolls with the leftover dough
helped with spelling

meatloaf and mashed potato mother
we had the World Book
a piano and a puppy

she said a marriage was better
if the man loved the woman
more than the woman loved the man

I think she wanted to be one of us
instead of the mother

wanted the man
who would love her more

THE FATE OF ROMANCE OVER TIME

I reach for the vestige of a younger me
in the pictures friends are always sending.
I can barely find her, illegible girl twirling
in a frothy green skirt, brown braids flying,
hot animal of her skin sewn into his, her
own thread disappearing. Holding a baby,
then another, she ruled her small world
uncaring how close her heart was
to the surface, how many times she climbed
into a smoking house sure that knowing
where the exits were would save her. I
want to turn her into Technicolor, teach her
to be truant from the school of foolishness,
show her the plain arithmetic of loss and love.
But instead I swipe forward, see her remnants
recede into the woman I retrieve this morning,
who whispers for transcendence into the ear
of the makeup gods. How I ache for her
flaming.

WHERE I COME FROM

I come from tantum ergo and holy mary mother of god and bless me father and long black robes I almost wore with the heavy cincture the wooden beads the deep pockets and those blue uniforms with white collars and cuffs we basted on each night after washing and ironing until I got smart and used snaps I'm from parents who never should have married who wanted me to be a boy and had no girl's name chosen parents who raged in the '50s ranch house my father built his American Dream I was not his American Dream I asked too many questions and I'm from all those questions and some of the answers many of which keep changing and morphing into more questions and I'm from the hold of a ship coming from Italy all the women screaming and praying my father and his sister Rose drinking wine from their nippled bottles and the great uncle a poet sent to Siberia his right arm cut off for writing his poems and now I write them and I'm from that apartment in Philadelphia where I tried making chicken salad in hollowed out pineapple shells correcting papers cleaning toilets feeding the baby carrots which he took in and in and in and then spit out all over me and now that baby is dead the seeds of death were in him already and though the other baby is still alive part of me is not and never will be and I'm no good at pretending that it will and that thin young man who saw me across the room in my kilt and loafers and wanted me and still wants me

THE NUNS TAUGHT US THE PERFECTION OF A MARTYR'S DEATH

if we died the day of our first communion
its exclusive state of grace
would take us straight to heaven

no stops for lunch
jump rope
first kiss

right into the everlasting
lap of God

like a suicide bomber
my friend said

yes, just like that

the pack of explosives
strapped to my white organdy waist
over the ruffle and the big bow
cinching my veil

gone girl
blown up for Him

LINES

I like things in lines, their benign design, lists, teeth, signs, rows of corn in the field by Route 7, stiff spines of shelved books. But not the lines around my eyes or those of frown on yours, when I'm out of line. *Get in line*, the nuns proclaimed, boys in one, girls in another, that line of thinking, dividing us more than we already were— scuffed shoes, our new breasts, straight line to heaven screwed by mixing? Queues of rights and wrongs, columns of sinners and saved we lived among. The bottom line she crossed that last morning.

RESHUFFLE

What a well I fell into
this morning, a door
in the wind, doubt
without faith, all that
childhood inside me.
Isn't there something
in us that can forget?
When love is over,
its ashy bits scattered,
we should stop wanting
all the things that never
happened, praying
sorrowful mysteries
again and again. I have
scissors, a knife, don't use
them. God of the ravaged,
do what they could do.

ANGLE

over the top
intense
excessive
too much
I stop
at all their
stations
but don't
get off
she said
extreme personality
destroyer of serenity
incendiary?
I won't
burn you
try to think
of me
as a warm hand
on your forehead

COOKIES

"How Eileen Myles, Poet, Spends Her Sundays"
—*New York Times*

Sunday night, and I'm
scooping small mounds
of dough onto metal sheets,
baking chocolate chip
cookies, while the *Times*
tells us that Eileen is
reading Elena Ferrante
or calling her lover in LA.
Somehow I'm sure she's
never baked one cookie,
while the sugary things
riddle my wife history.
Eileen is so cool, East
Village queer, poet before
there were downtown women
who did that sort of thing.
I like thinking about how
maybe I could have been
one too, run from the white
veil and groom, lived on
popcorn and wine for poems
and women. But everyone
loves cookies.

CHIAROSCURO

my friend Joan wants to know if my mother was
self-aware

we'd been talking about her death, how its thin bell
rings and rings in my life

how we make love up when it's not there

she smoked Phillip Morris, wouldn't let me
do as I say and not as I do

watched Bishop Sheen, Belafonte and Arnaz on TV
liked imaginary men the best

came to Rome with us when he died
but never cried

you'd be so much prettier if you got your eyelids done
she holds hers up to show me

if I lived in Nepal I'd have stood by a burning pyre
smelling her smoke
I'd be wearing white for a year

but I live here, sorting through her rugs and chairs
and dishes

she put things in compartments I said
sliced feelings into slivers to fit

no, she wasn't

EVERYBODY DOESN'T GET EVERYTHING

you were beginning to die
and we knew it

your body a withered waiting room

I loaned you my man for the job
you never gave him back

no way for me to taste the holy
in what was happening

seeing the past in my face
you wanted cheap grace

forgiveness without *I'm sorry*

a funeral in everything
even then

ASHES

She'd already lived too long, a hundred
years, even she had said it. I didn't want
her ashes. Especially not in a walnut box,
a silver locket, or teddy bear, the mortuary
choices. She was dead, and I was glad.
I was a bad mother, she'd say, fishing.
I didn't deny it. My best wounds came
from her. A girl on her knees, I'd buried
my song, trimmed my need, so she would
love me. She pushed me to be best, but
the music of applause was for both of us.
It's complex, I know, this mother-daughter
show. She tried her breasts, but nipples
never rose for me. We became such others
to each other, though she's sewn into my psyche.
The space between what could have been
and was is where I live.

REMAINS

You are strong but not tender. Words flung
at me, not the last but could have been. Mother
is near the end, small in her big bed. I say
nothing, wait to become an orphan. *Your soup
keeps me alive*, she says, fixing me with fierce
new eyes. She wants to die today, and that soup
makes it my fault that she hasn't. *Do you
believe I love you?* I lie. *Yes*, I say. And then,
Do you love me? Harder, but my family is listening,
and so I say *of course I do*. Bigger lie. How
could a daughter not love her mother? I want
to go to more of myself, and the next day I will
begin, sit alone in the room with her sad little
purse of bones and tell her what I couldn't say
while she lived.

NO ANSWER

All those years I sat at her table wanting
a bowl of fresh fruit, not the tough meat
of her tired nostrums—*love one another,*
there is nothing more important than love.
Such a hungry girl, I wanted to change
her into a woman who could live her words.
But starvation was tiring—I left for a good
man, a bad one would have let her own
me longer. Snacking on replacements
for her kept me stuck, a flailing girl-fish
too easily hooked. On and on she dissembled
until none of us knew what was true
anymore. The unsaid lodged in her scented
silk pillows and scarves, her thin china cups,
her shrinking body, became a cacophony
while we watched her die. *I'm writing about*
our mother, I say to my sister. *In a good way*
or a bad way? she asks. *In a real way,* I say.
Does it help? she wants to know.

TO THE VERY END

she put on lipstick, creamed her face, pulled
up her Talbot's pants, donned her J. Crew sweater.

Just the Ferragamos she couldn't, ankles, feet swollen
so only slippers fit. *You have a duty to look your best*

for the world, she taught me, what her mother
had taught her. Message I inherited, though

a slightly disheveled look was more my style.
You're wearing that? she said about my handmade

sandals, loose tunic bought in Taos I'd packed
for the mother-daughter weekend at the upstate retreat
center,

where no one wears makeup or Talbot's. She'd
agreed to come only if we got the one carpeted cabin.

I got it. *My daughter thinks I'm in denial*, she said
at the first meeting, smiling as she charmed the room.

How did it happen that the weekend I'd hoped
would help to heal us, became all about the years of silence

between her and my father? When we were told
to write notes of apology to each other, my mother penned

hers to him. Why had I dreamed the long wild howl
of our relationship could transform into a whisper
that weekend?

Even now that she's dead, I still hear it.

TIGER'S NEST HIKE, BHUTAN 2017

Alone on the stone steps, I can only keep
going. People rush at me, girls in flip-flops
and flats, two couples with babies, Indians
in turbans, women in kiras, men in ghos.
Do you know Fin? I ask men who look like
our guide, whom I have lost, along with
the group. They shake their heads no.
Get to the Buddha. Keep your eyes down
so you don't see up, watch the steps, hold
to the thick metal rail, small sips of water
only. An old thread in my soul pulls me ahead,
my mother's legacy, *keep going, move on,
no matter what*, she said as she painted white
over red, walls of blood our family spurted.
Teahouse? Teahouse? People point, a man offers
water, sees me sweating, mine almost gone.
Fin, when I get there, says I've worked off
some karma. But it's the words inside me
I need more to say *it's okay* if I'd stopped,
sat down on those stone stairs and sobbed,
given up, the words to say *it's okay,
I'll love you anyway.*

Two.

NIGHTFALL

tonight I hear it first
the small explosion

                      when our son
                      fell to his death

outside our window
splicing the dark

                      only the night
                      heard him

with a storm of stars
a tree, I thought

                      here
                      on the other side

a tree
falling on wires

                      I try
                      to imagine

we'd had rain
for weeks

                      what song
                      his body made

our huge
silver maple

                    meeting the Roman
                    earth, his hand

ninety years
it has stood

                    clutching
                    a sycamore branch

    behind our old house
    the gouge

                    I think something
                    maybe a tree

in its side
as big as his body

                    must have grown
                    in that sound

thick tumble
of trunk, bark, and branch

                    where he lay
                    weakening

so large
I cannot see

                    his blood seeding
                    the ground

I'm sorry for your loss

people still say but death is an old neighborhood now I've *gotten on with it* (haven't I) the sorrow that was the size of the ocean's exhale is less (isn't it) but feeling better makes me feel worse, the lavish wound unlocked with kindness *be kind for everyone you meet is carrying a great burden* and you can't know kindness really until you have known its lack, can you? I'd hoped death's room had given me all I'd needed—a careful scouring of hope, ground glass in every mouthful of its fetid air, but here's the winter/summer of your hair again, the morgue's starched white sheets, the smell of you in the Roman streets—all these years grief a guest that never leaves, so much practice in anguish, I've become more like myself—is it very hard to be dead? it's been hard to be alive *be kind for everyone you meet is carrying a great burden* you were so kind, giving Gabby your Irish sweater, lire to the homeless Romans, making me laugh with your bad jokes but I've idealized you I know *I'm sorry for your loss* after so many years I reach into the same box of exhausted memories pull out shreds of possibility but I really only know the story of me without

SHOULD HAVE

what everyone was afraid of I wasn't afraid of even though
I should have been, after all

you had almost died once, though I never would have
given what was happening in that hospital room

the name *dying*, oxygen monitor fastened on your finger
like the black clip I put on my manuscripts

about your death—I was stupid that week in a white shirt
splashed with colored leaves

your father and I too shocked by your gray face to shake
those doctors talking about the weather

while you gasped—he stayed with you all night, it was I
who went back to work

see, I couldn't have believed you'd die if I did that, got in
my car and drove to the office instead

of into bed with you, pushing my breath into your flaccid
lungs---the only ending to this story

is that I should have known and didn't, or that maybe
I should have tried harder

to keep you near but then you would have run farther
and died anyway

ABOUT THIS TIME OF YEAR

It's about this time of year we
would have gone, you wrangling
with your brother over who got to sit
in the front, me piloting the gray Torino
to Canaan. Bob's Clothing, the black block
letters spelled out over the storefront—
we pulled over and parked. Bob
greeted us at the door as if we were
visiting him at his home. You were
all smiles even though your brother
jostled you for first dibs at shoe try-ons.
Wally, who if he weren't Bob's only
salesperson would have been a homeless
man, brought out the boxes of blue
suede Pumas, white leather Adidas.
He always had the right size. Then the jeans—
Levis of course, three pairs each—
the gym shorts, were they Adidas too?
—French blue with three stripes down each side.
You wore them every day that summer.
Gray T-shirts, and white with a collar,
the little alligator, for good. I'd talked Bob
into stocking them for the Lakeville boys.
A plastic bag of tube socks each, underwear,
and jean jackets if last year's didn't fit. Bob
discounted everything, talking all the while,
wanting to be sure we had what we needed.
Big bags out to the car between you both

in the back seat now, me alone in the front—
we're all laughing, driving home past the drugstore,
the library, and the skating pond, the big
white church where we'd have your funeral
ten years later.

FOOL

I know nothing. Except this:
Death sticks to you, its flypaper
paws reach out to everything
you've ever loved—the Beatles
and the Doors, a soft bed, pasta
with Bolognese sauce. Even tulips.
Husbands. That book you read in 1987.
All gummy with remembrance.
And the pictures on the piano?
put them away. Foolish to say,
"You'll get over it." You won't.

VERSIONS

I don't want a new winter coat, a perfect
summer day, a grilled cheese sandwich.
To get to the end of this poem, my
dead son back. Well, I'm lying about
that. Unknowable music of what could be
and isn't. But who would I have become
without this wound? The same small
gray-hair I am now, I suppose. Injured
only by age, the usual human hungers.
The hollowing filled, the invisible visible.
The moment before his fall, just an ordinary
woman.

THERE IS ALWAYS A WOLF

after they empty you from your morgue-box
a dark-suited guard arrives

only one point of light in that room
starched white sheet that swaddles you

when your father dares move the sheet to see—what—
how broken you were from the fall

that guard banishes his hand

I've never fathomed what put him there
why we said nothing

not *this is our son, vattenne!*
his bones and skin belong to us

there is always a wolf

we held each other in that shadowy temple
I have called so many things love
and now this

BEHIND US

Cette ville est magnifique I write on each
postcard—we're using the last of the stamps.
Splendide, I say, *Merveilleuse*—

Tomorrow we leave, but now—*fromage*,
baguette, a demi of *vin rouge*, real tourists—
a picnic on a marble bench by the Seine.

It's clean here, no dirty condoms or tampon
wrappers—the French keep things up
better than the Italians.

Or maybe it's just where we are—maybe it's dirtier
downriver where tourists don't go—our dead son
probably woulld have liked that part better.

I'm in my new skinny jeans and black boots,
you're wearing the jacket we bought
in Montmartre the day it started to rain.

But today the sun is shining, the river gleams—
you hold the camera in front of us, snap a few photos.
We're happy here. We've forgotten the other wall,

the one by the Tiber he fell from, until later we see
this one behind us in the pictures—the stacked granite
blocks, my gray hair against the dance of leafy shadows.

Fifteen feet, I think, not fifty, this wall by the Seine—
you think a bit more. *He would have lived*, I say.
He would have lived.

THINGS

There's no more room on the storage shelves
your father built in the garage when we moved in.

None either in the cupboards, the pantry, the freezer,
the closets, the bookshelves or the garden. Everyone

else our age seems to be emptying—moving to condos
or senior living, giving things to their children,

thrift shops, having tag sales. Not me. I want my old
red house with all its groanings, damp basement, steep

stairs, so many things that need fixing. I want my
bedroom on the second floor with its chestnut beams

and the windows that look out on open fields. I want
all the clothes in my closet, the assemblage of suitcases

that suggest I will still be going places, the Kandinsky
poster from the Peggy Guggenheim that you brought

me when we had to leave Venice before it was open.
And I want you, my son dead these thirty-five years, how

I want you—more than all these other things, all the things
I've wanted but couldn't have, all the things I can have

but don't want. I'd live in an empty room if you'd come back.
But who would you be then, the boy who died or the man

you'd become? I wouldn't know you anymore. You wouldn't
know me, transformed all these years by your absence. Should

I still believe my thirst could be slaked, my life reshaped,
by your return?

DEATH

a box
into which
everything
must fit

CASUALTY

enough of blackbirds, bluebirds, sparrows, the pricey seeds
my husband fills feeders with, enough of the squirrels
and mice that eat them instead, enough of falling in love
and out, of what got us here, what will get us elsewhere,
enough of his leg, my back, lost friends, lost minds, enough
of me me me poor me, the dead mother, the never-enough
girl, our country 'tis of thee, purple mountains and fruited
plains, graphs and shootings, rising seas and men in suits,
senseless hope, confines of the body, murkiness of the soul,
forecasts of snow, detachment and prognosis, the night
between us, the absence of you.

Three.

For the longest time

I was only interested in love, how it owns you,
slices you open, throws you away, then corrals

you into its comfortable fence. The boy I loved
first didn't love me, and it's a good thing because

I heard from our old teacher that he killed himself
a few years ago. I think the problem was maybe

I was raised without tenderness so what I looked for
was more like suffering, mistaking wounds for salve.

The hard stories made sense to me. But then
there was you, and I didn't know what to do

with all that kindness, how to trust its soft safety,
how to return it, still wishing for a voice

like the one on my phone saying *turn left, turn right,
you have arrived at your final destination.*

THE WAY IT WAS
Southeast Asia, 2007

in a coma of someone else's lies
I stumble into lavish temples

light joss sticks
bow to golden Buddhas

shake dripping lotus flowers
over my head

our bathroom has red tile
outside the window, women hide

their faces from the sun
under cone-shaped hats

we shut the blinds
fall into each other

I wear my green silk *ao-dai*
to dinner

the girl is still running from napalm
I dream something is trying to kill me

you bring me tea
stroke my face

under pressed white sheets
we shimmer

RECKONING

Why didn't you tell me you were
drowning? I was so new to being pretty,
you, to saving yourself. Bitter liturgy
left behind. We went to the monastery
together this time, but the monks
were off-key, their song lacked life,
and we left. Saint Paul says it's better
to marry than to burn. But marriage
is incendiary too. Sticky, trembling, I
was not ready to be given away. So
many fires after the first, though I
never found a way to stay warm.

FAMINE

There is nothing new here, not in Sharkey's Pub,
the bleating sheep, gorse, or heather. Grass verges
along the roadside, chalk mountains, and Maghery
Beach in the rain. It's all the same, and so are we,
tease of blue sky, stone walls, and melancholy. We
reach for each other, but there's too much to hold,
days overlong, the roads wind nowhere, and it's
always cold. Bella's burro brays the morning open,
Mary Boyle asks us for tea, a piece and jam, comes
to us to eat fish stew without her husband. Her brother
died of the drink, eight more struggle. Ireland.
Donegal this time. Mary hungers for what she thinks
we have, she doesn't know we're starving too.

LISCANNOR, 2018

Sliver of sun somewhere, but mist
makes it Ireland. Up the road, then
down, lost amidst the lichen-splattered
stones stacked sidewards, tangled
hedgerows that offer berries too soon
to eat, can't find the yellow house
I live in now, Moira's house, where
the blue-robed virgin guards the door.
Roads have no names here, the sea
retreats, brown grasses long for green.
Let's imagine I stop hungering to find
my way, that I'd kept my mother's
ashes. Let's imagine I find flame,
mix mist and ash, pave another path.

ODE TO IRELAND

I'm hoarding me against you, Ireland,
Irish man I married. You'll have to take
an axe to my hard coat. I want to run
from you, go to Naples or Rome, where
I fit, small tan woman nothing like your
fair, freckled femmes. No fairy trees for me,
hazel bush to tie a white rag around, make
a wish, pray to it. Your bog got me once,
mucked my boots, sucked me down.
Your wind nearly knocked me off a cliff.
Your rain trained me to resist, I'm not
giving in now. Not to your splendid cloud
clusters, your extraordinary landscapes,
beetroot salads or poet men with turquoise shirts
the color of the covers of their books. Oh no,
you can't feed me with Heaney, Yeats,
or Kavanaugh. Not Derick Mahon, John
Fitzgerald, even Evan Boland. I can't let
myself love you, I'll dissolve if I do. Like
the first time I kissed a woman and just
knew. But fastened my mask a little tighter,
after all I had to live in the world I'd made,
sing its safe song. Still do.

WIFE

I'm not very good at loving you,
uncivilized over the morning eggs,
indifferent to your newly risen
kohlrabi and kale, greedy for what
you can't give me, forgetting to be
grateful for all you do. *Brutal happiness*,
my friend Glen said about marriage—
maybe she meant you get the worst
of me, my tired cargo of regrets
and re-windings but that I still
remember your skin is tender. We
hold the history of grief and living,
the silver and turquoise ring you put
under my pillow that night, the twisted
gold at the bottom of my Christmas
stocking. The boys our bodies made,
one gray-haired now, one dead, all five
of our black labs, dancing at the Plaza,
building the barn. Your fixed heart,
my mended back. I broke a date
with a nice guy to say yes to you
that first time. You told me later
if I'd said no, you would have given
me a second chance.

WIFE, AGAIN

Bake cakes, fold sheets, scrub tubs,
have a baby, then another, what a wife
should do. Try out marital equipment:
how to abide in wreckage, tangled lyrics
of love and loss. Not like the movies,
and she's always thirsty, it snows, and she
doesn't know what she doesn't know.
It goes on like that for years and then
more snow. She pleads guilty, but some
doors she never opens. The thing about
love: you starve without it. The places
that scare her are more and loud,
and the babies become men, and one
falls a long way down, and she wants
someone to slip a note under the door
saying *I'll save you,* but no one does.

HOSTAGE

I've been feeling peeled, like a fruit
that needed a sharp knife. Ripped,
like the final gash in old cloth
already frayed, whispering in the dark
for soothing from something I'm not
ready to call god. The world is breaking,
and I'm breaking with it. White men
in black suits making hell on earth. I
thought I'd seen the end of that,
what man can do to man, to woman.
Auschwitz, Birkenau, the Killing Fields,
bones and teeth on gritty paths, mounds
of shoes and suitcases, cyanide cans,
typed lists, numbered photographs.
Shouldn't it all be history?
I'm too angry for metaphors, too scared
for rhyme. Ravaged unmothered earth
we live on now. I want to have a bottom
line, a limit to what I can bear, a scream
that says *enough*, a key to tenderness.

NEED TO EXHALE

Another slaughter, junk of it all,
the gutted playgrounds, blown-up

apartments, hospitals and schools,
lost birthday parties, wrecked weddings.

The absence of mercy. Bodies in Bucha.
Blasted bridges, broken dams,

vile irony of *Arbeit macht frei*,
Auschwitz, place where birds couldn't sing.

Tuol Sleng, the Killing Fields, stacks of skulls
in a tall glass stupa, the erased ones,

their photographs in the museum
we went to, grim catalogue in black and white.

Now Gaza, the Jews, barbed wire in the mouth,
burst flesh of babies, whole country a deathbed.

I long for another story, sickened
by the language of these.

There's too much to mourn,
but still the trees

will burst leaves in the spring, flowers
will break through the bloody soil.

THE ELECTRICIAN

I was twenty-two, married a month,
didn't even know I was pregnant.

He'd come to repair the broken
light in the bathroom, the switch
in the bedroom—a ponderous, pasty
man, gray hair, could have been
a grandfather.

I was correcting papers in
the kitchen. He said he was
finished, would I check his
work?

There was a stained glass
window by the sink, coral
tile, a big tub. I pulled the
switch—*yes, it's fine*—

And then he was on me,
his hard swelling against me,
my baby.

Some new voltage in my
body screamed and pushed—
get off, get out—

This time he pinned me, head
against the tub, my knee hit
hard, he crawled to the door.

I'm sobbing, dripping from his pawing touch, such a big man, such big hands.

The lights were fixed, but no one believed me. The landlord said *his son is in law school.*

It was 1964. No men did things like that.

THE BOSS CHOOSES ME

I want to eat a whole box of chocolates,
drink a quart of wine, read *The New York Times*,
anything but dive into this damage. There's
no way to tell this well, the story's too old,
the shame's too great for metaphor.

why

didn't you call me my husband said when I told him. I would have come for you. And he would have, but another man had already offered to rescue me. Okay I said maybe he was different didn't just want what the others had wanted, their hands under my sweater or T-shirt or dress and then the next place. And I thought I was brave to stay where I was. He followed me to the beach lunch and dinner and then to my small cabin that had no lock, and he said please, and I said no and no again maybe not loud enough, and then I was on the floor not rape really   was it.

SIMULACRUM

sometimes
I put the key in
and it won't
turn
I wanted
a warm room
not just
flesh

STICKY RICE

I should be happy here, amidst the glittering
cornucopia of the young, their clear skin,
smooth cheeks, constant din. But who needs
me? They surely don't. My sexual hunger
extinguished while their satedness screams
in my face. In any case, I distrust kindness.
Someone who likes me, I suspect for bad taste.
Once, in the jungle, I saw a tapir and forgot
everything before and after. I want to feel
that again, like the morning I fed the monks,
put balls of sticky rice into their bronze bowls
before the sun came up. Couldn't the god
of sadness not get reelected? Once I loved
with everything in my purse, all my furniture,
even my car. The sadness god says sorry, I'm
staying on, and you should have known this
would be all you'd get.

.

ALMOST

What adhered us shouted louder
than the beeps and hisses of those machines
around you. You'd been dead two hours,
now you'd come alive again, rib halves
wired back, tubes and tape all over you,
fixed heart beating in regular rhythm.
Our son and I hung somewhere in the noise,
inconsequential cogs in the cathedral
of human repair. It was sunny, that May
day, we'd sat in the shine of it while they
mended you. The brightness belied
what was happening inside, it sheltered us
when we wondered if we'd heard your last
words. But no. I wouldn't have to organize
my life around another death, though I'd
been ready to become a widow. I owe
someone something for this, tenderness
of reclamation. Your name wouldn't
have to be crossed out, the world will
still have us in it.

I KNOW YOU CAN'T HEAR ME

I'd like to be
younger but
fire doesn't choose
to burn the wood
and sometimes
there is no fire
sometimes
there is no wood
you need both
don't you
and I don't really mean
I want to be younger
just not this old
feeling in the dark
for a door in the wind
a line in the water
invisible
peripheral
ringing
a thin bell

THE THINGS I CARRY

two fragments of bone in a blue leatherette folder, the ticket stub from the Red Sox game I went to with my son, three packs of Kleenex, the letter that said *I am nothing and will only become more nothing*, the Roman morgue, the steps down to the Tiber

I carry the room I shared with my sister and the Saint Anthony statue on our turquoise bureau, hundreds of rosaries and novenas, canasta games with Diane Amidon, Patty Turner's driveway

I carry hair gels and sprays and volumizing shampoo, one husband, two wedding rings, an extra thong, Chinese herbs, and always, Advil, I carry intensity though I don't want to, and fear though it's wearing a raincoat and you can't see it

I carry pounds of bracelets and a chocolate bar, jeans that don't fit, uncertainty and potential, I carry drama though my husband says *love is not drama* it doesn't seem quite right without it

I don't carry peace although I should

I carry the memory of my little boys at the table drawing in our first house, the sun shining on their hair as they bent over their pads, a fall day, pie in the oven, stew on the stove

I carry the glass half-full, five black labs, the sure knowledge of my death, metal in my lower back, questions with no answers, I carry apples, every luscious bite

CAN THIS MARRIAGE BE SAVED?

Light comes and goes in the story of us.
Out here in Wyoming, the deer are different,

and I don't know the names of the birds,
but I do know I am happy without you.

This landscape forgives me my sins, too huge
for them to matter though someone has hung

skulls on the cottonwoods, path by the creek
I walk every day. But soon I will return to our

bed and the dog, the Amazon packages, the dead
dahlias. We've been assigned to each other,

you said marriage was a one-way ticket
with no transfers, remember? That throng

of fantasies we shared, a plunder. You try
to teach me mortal lessons, I walk ahead

of you, believing I have no need of salvation.
But when I can't open a jar or figure out why

my car won't start, I immediately imagine
what life would be like as a widow. Things

seem so singular out here, but then I see sheep
flocked, birds charging each other in the wide sky,

think how necessary it is to belong somewhere,
how I belong to you.

ECLIPSE

for Ricardo
Big Horn, 2021

The bigger of the two men I'm with, the one wearing
the cowboy hat, blue eyes that lash me to his with a piercing

that captivates—clasps my waist with his large hands
so tightly I'm afraid I might fly as he lifts me

to the next snowy ridge. *I'll throw you over my shoulder
and carry you*, he says, those eyes fixing me steadily, and I vanish

into his need for rescue, mine for strength. How effortlessly
I become the distressed damsel, my years of fight floundering—

so when I wake screaming that night—huge hands had me
pinned, held me down—I knew—I mean, I knew everything—

all my furious history streaming back—*Breathe*, he'd said,
through the nose, out the mouth, my lungs slack, my legs

sudden jelly—in the dream the man had his hands on my sex
—maybe *I thought I had to, I thought I had to*—

and okay, maybe I'd wanted to—hey, just for an afternoon—
but there are other men, with gentler hands.

DONE

I'll save you, he said. Touch
like a match that starts the flame,
those days of bad decisions.
So much easier to not want—
breasts rest quiet in their cups,
amygdala, id, whatever it is
that sweeps the need for rescue
into someone else's arms, asleep.
Better that I butter toast, brew
coffee, make stews and soups,
slice apples for a pie. No need
to lie or tell truth that stings.
Explorer in a new world,
both feet in.

JUST THIS FACT

I was on the train when the doctor's note
came in. *Shadow in a place it shouldn't be—*
Because it was a weekend and nothing
could have been done anyway, we stayed
in the city. My friend brought me a totem
necklace she'd made from leather and bead,
my husband's eyes looked grim. I couldn't
focus on the play, the art, imagining how
the end would come, the pain before. Such
a clean time, the mess of the rest of life
exiled, just this fact of something that would
kill me. Home, another ultrasound. A bad
read, the other, a mistake, nothing wrong,
only the fatality of such ferocious clarity.

NO ONE'S GETTING ANYTHING RIGHT EXCEPT THE TREES

Clearmont, Wyoming, 2021
I see more sky here than I ever have,
in fact, I'm almost too full of it, stuffed
with space and bright October snow.
The cottonwoods outside my window
don't have to try to be alive, they just are,
unlike me, for years blurred by suffering
and sorrow. In space free of savage memory,
I strive to learn a new taxonomy—sacks
of wrong facts I must discard, old dry dates
reject. Ravaged yesterdays, my own
and theirs, those with skins of different
colors than my white one. Who measures
grief? Here on land that belongs to others,
what should we want to love? Redo it all
I say, wound repair for history, but how?
I only know abstractions are distractions,
but action can, and kindness. The world
can't be saved with a syllabus.

COMPOST

I grow things now. Cleome, angelica, rudbeckia,
Russian sage, dahlias, verbena bonariensis.
But it's the weeding I love best. In my overalls
for hours, I clip, pull, rake, stake, dirt on my knees,
my hands, stung, sunburned, I keep at it despite
mold on the phlox, beetles on the rosebush,
hydrangeas that have no buds again this year.
I curse the deer who ate half the hosta last night,
daylily buds and zinnias for dessert. *They'll come
back*, my husband says. *Plants have their own design,
death is part of it, resilience too. You have to understand
survival.* Isn't that what I've been trying to do, staying
alive all these years since our son died, I think but
don't say. Instead, careful not to disturb the beetles,
I pick some flowers, make a bouquet.

THIRD AGE

The great damp beast of need
recedes, furls up the flag

of sorrow, thinned by loss,
cargo tossed, arias instead

of threnody. Point of passion
now to simply stay alive, door

neither opening nor closing.
Raised on worry, war, white

bread, we ate the ordinary
pie life gave us, thought

we knew the big city of love,
faith, faithlessness. The time

is not right to love less. Now
that we know what comes

next, let's ingest some artless
happiness.

ANSWER

Let's imagine I could come up with one.
I've been saved and savior, loved

and left and loved again. Warm beast
of desire cooled, innocence and drama

exiled, flames frozen over. I dove in,
dove in deeper, and didn't drown.

Tools of my history, these words, grief
the ghost that lingers. Softer footprints

now. So many years of not-enough
and now enough. What's after

making love? A woman the subject
of her own story.

Acknowledgments

"Almost," Finalist, *Broad River Review*, 2021 Rash Awards
"Can This Marriage Be Saved," *One Art*, August 2022
"Casualty," *One Art*, August 2022
"Chiaroscuro," *Mothers and Mentors: The Art of Nurturing*, Story Circle Network, 2023
"Cookies," *Mudfish*, Vol. 21, 2020
"for the longest time," *Broad River Review*, 2024 Rash awards, finalist
"Famine," *Upstreet*, 2018
"Hostage," Second Prize, 2021 Nutmeg Poetry Contest, CT Poetry Society, *CT River Review*
"I'm sorry for your loss," *The Halcyone, Sixty-Four Best Poets of 2018*, Black Lawrence Press
"No Answer," *The Halcyone, Sixty-Four Best Poets of 2018*, Black Lawrence Press
"Ode to Ireland," First Prize, 2021 *Story Circle Network* Poetry Contest
"Paper Dolls," Honorable Mention, 2011 *Passager* Poetry Contest

"Remains," Third Prize, 2021 *Story Circle Network* Poetry Contest

"Should Have," *Rhino*, Spring 2025

"The Electrician," *Naugatuck River Review*, 2023 contest, semi-finalist

"The Things I Carry," *Italian Americana*, Winter 2022

"Things," *The Comstock Review*, Spring 2022

"Where I Come From," *Italian Americana*, 40.1 Fall 2022

"Wife," *Poet Lore*, Vol. 115, Spring/Summer 2020

"why," *Passenger Journal*, Winter 2022

"Reshuffle" and "Hostage," from *Unhinged*, Sharon Charde, Blue Light Press, 2019

"Things" and "Where I Come From" nominated for 2022 Pushcart prizes

A large thank-you to all these journals for publishing my work. I am also deeply grateful to my dearest teachers over the years: Sharon Olds, Brenda Hillman, Marie Howe, Ellen Bass, Eileen Myles, and Natalie Goldberg. Without all their support and mentorship at very difficult times in my life, I'd never be who I am today.

Title Index

A
ABOUT THIS TIME OF YEAR 40
ALMOST 66
ANGLE 26
ANOTHER MOTHER 20
ANSWER 76
ASHES 30

B
BEHIND US 45

C
CAN THIS MARRIAGE BE SAVED? 69
CASUALTY 48
CHIAROSCURO 28
COMPOST 74
COOKIES 27

D
DEATH 47
DONE 71

E
ECLIPSE 70
EVERYBODY DOESN'T GET EVERYTHING 29

F
FAMINE 53
FOOL 42
For the longest time 50

H
HOSTAGE 58

I
I KNOW YOU CAN'T HEAR ME 67
I'm sorry for your loss 38

J
JUST THIS FACT 72

L
LINES 24
LISCANNOR, 2018 54

N
NEED TO EXHALE 59
NIGHTFALL 36
NO ANSWER 32
NO ONE'S GETTING ANYTHING RIGHT
   EXCEPT THE TREES 73
NORA DENNIS IS PRAYING FOR ME 19

O
ODE TO IRELAND 55

P
PAPER DOLLS 16

R
RECKONING 52
REMAINS 31

RESCUE 18
RESHUFFLE 25

S

SHOULD HAVE 39
SIMULACRUM 64
STICKY RICE 65

T

THE BOSS CHOOSES ME 62
THE ELECTRICIAN 60
THE FATE OF ROMANCE OVER TIME 21
THE NUNS TAUGHT US THE
    PERFECTION OF A MARTYR'S DEATH 23
THERE IS ALWAYS A WOLF 44
THE THINGS I CARRY 68
THE WAY IT WAS 51
THINGS 46
THIRD AGE 75
TIGER'S NEST HIKE, BHUTAN 2017 34
TO THE VERY END 33

V

VERSIONS 43

W

WHAT'S AFTER MAKING LOVE 13
WHERE I COME FROM 22
why 63
WIFE 56
WIFE, AGAIN 57

First Line Index

A
a box 47
after they empty you from your morgue-box 44
All those years I sat at her table wanting 32
Alone on the stone steps, I can only keep 34
Another slaughter, junk of it all 59

B
Bake cakes, fold sheets, scrub tubs 57

C
Cette ville est magnifique I write on each 45
Clearmont, Wyoming, 2021 73

D
didn't you call me my husband said when I told 63

E
enough of blackbirds, bluebirds,
    sparrows, the pricey seeds 48
Every day, she says. I want to say 19

I

I come from tantum ergo and
    holy mary mother of god 22
I'd like to be 67
I don't want a new winter coat, a perfect 43
I do want to be loved, to become 18
if we died the day of our first communion 23
I grow things now. Cleome, angelica, rudbeckia 74
I know nothing. Except this 42
I like things in lines 24
I'll save you, he said. Touch 71
I'm hoarding me against you, Ireland 55
I'm not very good at loving you 56
in a coma of someone else's lies 51
I reach for the vestige of a younger me 21
I should be happy here, amidst the glittering 65
It's about this time of year we 40
I've been feeling peeled, like a fruit 58
I've traded my pretty body enough to know 13
I want to eat a whole box of chocolates 62
I was only interested in love, how it owns you 50
I was on the train when the doctor's note 72
I was twenty-two, married a month 60

L

Let's imagine I could come up with one 76
Light comes and goes in the story of us 69

M

Mother dropped me 16
my friend Joan wants to know if my mother was 28

O

over the top 26

P

people still say but death is an
    old neighborhood now I've 38

S

sang with Frank, knew the words 20
She'd already lived too long, a hundred 30
she put on lipstick, creamed her face, pulled 33
Sliver of sun somewhere, but mist 54
sometimes 64
Sunday night, and I'm 27

T

The bigger of the two men I'm with, the one wearing 70
The great damp beast of need 75
There is nothing new here, not in Sharkey's Pub 53
There's no more room on the storage shelves 46
tonight I hear it first 36
two fragments of bone in a blue leatherette folder 68

W

What adhered us shouted louder 66
What a well I fell into 25
what everyone was afraid of
    I wasn't afraid of even though 39
Why didn't you tell me you were 52

Y

You are strong but not tender. Words flung 31
you were beginning to die 29

www.ingramcontent.com/pod-product-compliance
Lightning Source LLC
Chambersburg PA
CBHW010046090426
42735CB00020B/3413